TO:

FROM:

LEARNING

STEPS TO BECOMING A PASSIONATE LIFELONG LEARNER

By Russell Sarder

Russell Sarder
www.RussellSarder.com

Sarder Inc.,
20 West 33rd Street, 4F,
New York, NY 10001
www.sarder.com

Ordering information for quantity sales: Special discounts are available on quantity purchases by corporations, associations, and others. For details, contact the publisher at the address above.

Orders by U.S. trade bookstores and wholesalers:
Please contact Big Distribution: Tel: (646) 747-5410;
or e-mail to russell@netcomlearning.com

Printed in the United States of America
First Printing: 2011 April
ISBN: 978-0-9833788-2-2

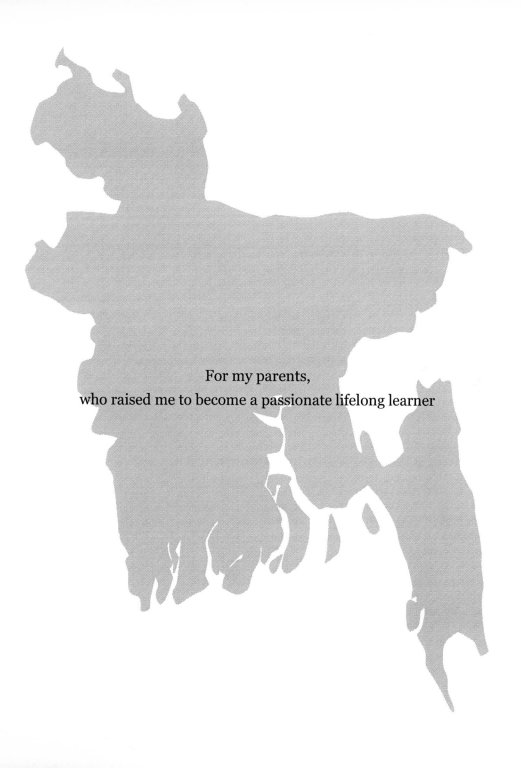

For my parents,
who raised me to become a passionate lifelong learner

"Live as if you were to die tomorrow.

Learn as if you were to live forever."

—Gandhi

TABLE OF CONTENTS

INTRODUCTION

Love of learning has dominated my life—it's at the center of my career as CEO of NetCom Learning, and it's how I spend my spare time. This is no surprise, since I'm my father's son, a man who has always been passionate about learning and possesses a tremendously curious mind.

When I was a boy in Bangladesh, he returned home from a long day as the director of a local hospital, not to lie on the couch or watch television, but to read late into the night—a dozen newspapers, along with piles of books.

"You'll ruin your eyes!" my mother used to tell him.

But my father was well aware of how much knowledge there was in the world, and how important it was to partake of it. And I have followed in his footsteps.

Learning is not only vital for success in life and business, it is also physically and mentally beneficial. When we learn, the connections between our brain cells grow stronger, and new pathways are etched onto our brains. To keep the neurons of the brain alive and vital, a person should learn something new each day. It turned out my parents were far ahead of their time in promoting the importance of continual learning for a successful life.

I've gathered this book of learning quotes in order to inspire others as my father inspired me.

In my own life, I have always wanted to create a learning movement, not only in my corporation and home, but also in the entire country. This is a promising and crucial time to promote lifelong learning. With high unemployment and increased competition due to globalization from technological changes, old skills are becoming obsolete. In order to remain competitive in this changing environment, all of us need to continue learning.

I love reading quotation books because I find them an inspiring way to learn how people have become successful. But as I researched, I was unable to locate a book that focused on learning, nor one that linked an author's biography with his or her inspiring words. And so I decided to write one myself.

I initially began with thousands of quotes from illustrious people, both past and present, whose lives have exemplified excellence and achievement. I read the words of industry leaders, presidents, educators, authors, and politicians from every era. When I had assembled the most compelling quotes, I linked each to one of the eight steps that I consider vital for becoming a passionate learner. These are:

STEP 1. LEARNING VALUE: Appreciate the value of attaining continuous knowledge.

STEP 2. LEARNING COMMITMENT: Embrace being a committed lifelong learner.

STEP 3. LEARNING ATTITUDE: Develop the right attitude towards continuous learning.

STEP 4. LEARNING PLAN: Develop the right attitude towards continuous learning.

STEP 5. LEARNING METHOD: Become an effective learner by combining a variety of learning methods.

STEP 6. READING: Read an hour each day and grow wealthy.

STEP 7. LIBRARY: **Build your own library.**

STEP 8. LEARNING APPLICATION: **Apply what you have learned.**

These eight learning steps have also been printed on handy cards; I hope you will hand them out to eight coworkers or friends.

Learning is more crucial than ever for achieving a productive life and career. I hope these quotes will inspire you as they have me. I ask you to join me in a new learning movement that will insipire a needed shift in our culture's attitude toward learning.

This book is a perfect gift for employees, children, grandchildren, graduates—anyone you care about and want to inspire.

Steps to Becoming a Passionate Lifelong Learner

Learning Value — Appreciate the value of attaining continuous knowledge.

Learning Commitment — Embrace being a committed lifelong learner.

Learning Attitude — Develop the right attitude towards continuous learning.

Learning Plan — Develop an effective learning plan to excel in your field.

Learning Method — Become an effective learner by combining a variety of learning methods.

Reading — Read an hour each day and grow wealthy.

Library — Build your own library.

Learning Application — Apply what you have learned.

Source: Sarder Inc. 2011

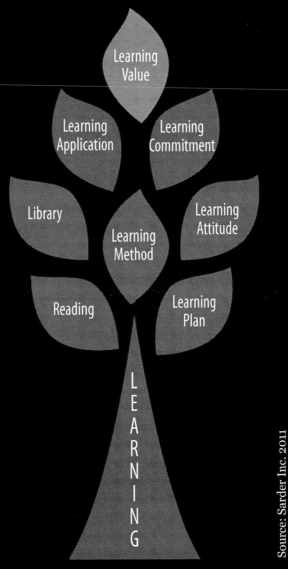

Steps to becoming a passionate lifelong learner

Source: Sarder Inc. 2011

STEP 1.
LEARNING VALUE

Appreciate the Value of
Attaining Continuous
Knowledge.

Unlike the value of a car or house, the value of lifelong learning is intrinsic. It is important in and of itself. You can't place a price tag on it. But that doesn't mean it won't vastly enrich your life.

I have an employee who worked for me five years, but in an earlier life had been a successful lawyer. He'd managed to acquire all the accoutrements that are part of the good life—a late model car, a lovely home. The problem was, these luxuries didn't make up for the feeling of boredom he felt each day as he spent his hours embroiled in case law.

So why had he gone into this field of work? The answer's easy, and not uncommon; it was the work his parents desired for him. He'd respected and loved his parents, so he had tried hard to follow the path they suggested. But now, in midlife, he was a parent himself and felt it was time to follow his own desires. And what he was really passionate about was information technology and teaching.

He didn't simply quit his legal job, but began taking courses and reading whatever he could get his hands on. At his law firm, he switched focus, establishing initial databases and creating systems to employ new IT functions. He discovered that each time he learned something new, it led to another topic he wanted to explore.

Soon he was teaching courses for free with other instructors, so that he could learn from them. He took classes at NetCom Learning for months to become certified in the areas he wished to teach, and went through our training program. Finally, he underwent an internship in our networking division, so that he could receive valuable hands-on training.

He ended up becoming one of the best trainers at NetCom Learning, so successful in fact that Microsoft recognized him after five years of training as one of the best technical instructors in different networking related products. And he is now making more money as a high-end technical trainer than as a lawyer.

Learning is the great liberator.

Houses can be foreclosed; the valuation of gold can rise and fall. But no one can take away the value of knowledge. It gives you a competitive edge; it enlarges your world. In my colleague's case, it changed his life.

You can't place a price tag on its value.

I have carefully selected the following quotes and biographies of ten successful people who have understood and appreciated the value of lifelong learning.

20

Learning Values related Quotes

Quotes and Biographies of Successful People Who Appreciate the Value of Lifelong Learning

BILL CLINTON
(b.1946)
42ND PRESIDENT OF THE UNITED STATES OF AMERICA

BILL CLINTON credits his grandmother, a strong-willed disciplinarian, with shaping his character and teaching him to become a very early reader, a habit that has benefited him throughout his life. When he lost a race for Governor of Arkansas in 1980, he read over 300 books and revamped himself for a second run, winning back his seat. Clinton would go on to become one of the best-read presidents the United States has ever known.

Clinton was so widely recognized as a voracious reader— reading fifteen to twenty books each month—that when he was president, the media often reported on what he was currently reading.

One journalist quipped that Clinton, "Always seems to be living a hundred lives at once compared to the rest of us." The journalist wasn't certain whether the lengthy list of books he'd received was a month's reading for Clinton or only a day's worth.

In today's knowledge-based economy, what you earn depends on what you learn.

—Bill Clinton

B.B. KING
(b.1925)
MUSICIAN

OFTEN THE best education comes from example, and B.B. King is proof of that. He understood the value of role models and paid attention to the teachers who graced his life. Character was learned from his mother, honor and a work ethic from the white farmer he worked for in his youth. He learned black pride from an early teacher, and basic guitar playing from his minister. Listening to the recordings of blues greats like Blind Lemon Jefferson introduced him to the blues guitar.

B.B.'s distinctive guitar style has been described as a combination of blues, gospel, and jazz, but it may be his influence on the development of the rock and roll guitar style that is most recognizable. Just as he relied on musical role models, he has been a role model for generations of electrical guitar players. He has received a Grammy Lifetime Achievement Award and the Presidential Medal of Freedom.

The beautiful thing about learning is that no one can take it away from you.

—B.B. King

DORIS LESSING
(b.1919)
AUTHOR & NOBEL PRIZE WINNER IN LITERATURE

GROWING UP in a mud and thatch cottage in colonial Africa, Doris Lessing later recalled that her home was nevertheless filled with books. Colonial white schools were a trial to Lessing, and she left school at the age of thirteen, choosing instead to self-educate. The arrival of books by mail was a cause for celebration, and she read whatever was available: Dickens, Kipling, Tolstoy, and D.H. Lawrence.

Lessing left home at fifteen to work as a nursemaid and started writing stories. She moved to London in 1949 and published her first novel, *The Grass is Singing*, the same year. She has written dozens of books, as well as plays, nonfiction, and autobiography. She won the Nobel Prize for Literature at age 87 in 2007, the oldest person to do so. Passionate about social and political issues, she inspired a generation of women with *The Golden Notebook*, which explores the inner life of women.

That is what learning is. You suddenly understand something you've understood all your life, but in a new way.

—Doris Lessing

ANTHONY J. D'ANGELO
SPEAKER & AUTHOR, CHICKEN SOUP FOR THE COLLEGE SOUL

ANTHONY J. D'Angelo teaches young people how to appreciate the value of their college experience. As a student at West Chester University in Pennsylvania, he was president of the student government. He loved college and wanted to help other young people have the same rewarding experience. He spoke his youthful words of wisdom about college life into a tape recorder. The result was his version of the College Blue Book, filled with advice for college students about how to get the most out of going to college.

In 1995, at the age of 23, he left his job to interview over 5,000 college students and 1,000 university professionals to discover why so many students were getting degrees without achieving an education. To address the problem, he created Collegiate EmPowerment, which provides seminars and inspirational materials for college students and higher educational professionals.

Develop a passion for learning. If you do, you'll never cease to grow.

—Anthony J. D'Angelo

Benjamin Franklin
(1706–1790)
Renaissance Man & Founding Father of the United States

One biographer called Benjamin Franklin "a harmonious human multitude" because of all that he could do and all that he had accomplished. He was a crowd all by himself: inventor, diplomat, publisher and writer, philosopher, entrepreneur, international celebrity, revolutionary, and more. He was also a volunteer organizer, par excellence, founding the first American public library, and organizing fire-fighting clubs and a public hospital.

Franklin was a pragmatist, who believed that hard work led to success and that it was a path open to anyone. This philosophy formed the basis for the idea of the "American Dream." Franklin also believed that a person could succeed in life and business by being virtuous, so he established a regimen of thirteen virtues that he followed. He continually sought new ways to better himself, whether morally, physically, or intellectually.

The investment in knowledge pays the best interest.

—Benjamin Franklin

CARL T. ROWAN
(1925–2000)
JOURNALIST & COMMENTATOR

CARL T. Rowan's autobiography is entitled *Breaking Barriers,* which is exactly what he did throughout his lifetime. Growing up under southern Jim Crow laws, he was nevertheless dedicated to pursuing an education. Rowan was class president and valedictorian of his high school, a graduate of Oberlin College, and earned his M.A. in Journalism from the University of Minnesota.

His education and intellect carried him far. He was one of the first African-Americans to serve as a commissioned officer in the Navy. While first and foremost a journalist, he served in the presidential administrations of Kennedy and Johnson in capacities ranging from Deputy Assistant Secretary of State to Director of the U.S. Information Agency. He was the first African-American to hold a seat on the National Security Council. For many years, he was a syndicated columnist for the Chicago Sun-Times and the Washington Post, often writing on race relations.

The library is the temple of learning, and learning has liberated more people than all the wars in history.

—Carl T. Rowan

Francis Bacon
(1561–1626)
English Statesman, Philosopher, and Father of the Scientific Method

Francis Bacon entered Trinity College of Cambridge at the youthful age of twelve. His course of study was typically medieval and conducted in Latin, and it convinced him that the science and method of the time were all wrong. Although an important political and legal figure of his day, Bacon's lasting importance is as a scientist and philosopher.

As a believer in progress, Bacon stood at the early beginnings of the modern era. He asserted that a scientific investigator must free his mind from false assumptions and not base science on belief and tradition. Repeated observation of nature by means of careful strategies was the way to determine scientific facts, according to Bacon's new approach. His arguments marked an important stage in the development of modern scientific method.

Knowledge is power.

—Francis Bacon

Malcolm S. Forbes
(1919–1990)
Publisher of Forbes Magazine

Malcolm Forbes was the long-time publisher of Forbes Magazine, founded in 1917 by his Scottish immigrant father to feature the "doers and doings" of capitalist America.

A graduate of Princeton, Forbes was known for his business acumen. He dabbled in politics, serving in the New Jersey Senate and losing a governor's race before taking over the family magazine.

As publisher, Forbes was an innovator who brought diversification. Under his management, the magazine grew steadily in size and prestige.

The New York Times euologized Forbes, calling him "his magazine's greatest merchandising tool, especially as financial journalism expanded to report on the personalities behind American business." He began the "Forbes 400," an annual list of the richest people in America and a satire on the "Fortune 500" list of the nation's top companies.

Education's purpose is to replace an empty mind with an open one.

—Malcolm S. Forbes

Ralph Waldo Emerson
(1803–1882)
American Transcendentalist Poet, Philosopher, Lecturer, and Essayist

EMERSON ENTERED Harvard College at the age of fourteen. In his junior year, he began to keep a list of the books he had read, as well as a journal that he would keep for the next fifty-five years. The thoughts registered in his journal became public lectures, and later, published essays.

Although he started out as a Unitarian minister, Emerson became disillusioned and left the ministry. In large measure, he supported himself as a popular lecturer. His influence was felt in all cultural circles of his time, extending from Walt Whitman to Louisa May Alcott. It was on Emerson's land that Thoreau was staying when he wrote his famous book, *Walden*. Emerson gave voice to an independent American identity based on self-reliance. He preached that Americans should not look back to the European past, or to inherited ideas and beliefs, but find within themselves the will and the reasons to act.

There is no knowledge that is not power.

—Ralph Waldo Emerson

THOMAS FULLER
(1608–1661)
ENGLISH CLERGYMAN & HISTORIAN

THE SON of a minister, Thomas Fuller spent his own career in the Anglican Church, but he was also one of the first English-speaking authors to be able to make a living through his writing. Fuller matriculated at Queens College, Cambridge, at the age of twelve. In only a few years, he had obtained both his B.A. and M.A. He held a succession of church positions, for the most part with increasing success. During the British Civil War, he was somewhat unwillingly the chaplain to a wartime regiment, where he had to focus his attention on staying alive.

"All that time I could not live to study, who did only study to live," he later said. He bemoaned losing his library and his manuscripts, but he was able to end his career as "Chaplain Extraordinary" to Charles II.

Known for his ready wit, tremendous knowledge derived from extensive reading, and prodigious memory, Fuller was a prolific writer of histories.

Learning makes a man fit company for himself.

—Thomas Fuller

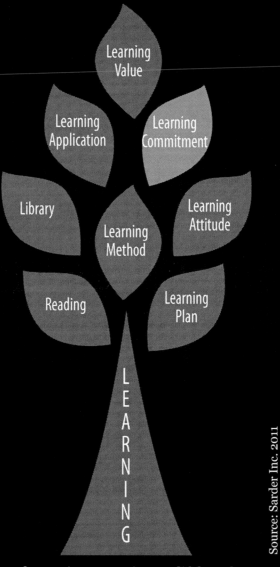

Learning Value

Learning Application

Learning Commitment

Library

Learning Method

Learning Attitude

Reading

Learning Plan

LEARNING

Source: Sarder Inc. 2011

Steps to becoming a passionate lifelong learner

Step 2.
Learning Commitment

Embrace Being a Committed
Lifelong Learner.

Commitment is the second step in becoming a passionate lifelong learner. It requires an adherence to excellence. It is a pledge you make to yourself. But before you can become committed, you have to know what you are passionate about, what excites and drives you.

I have an employee who worked for me for over ten years as a software developer, but it didn't fulfill him. Being involved all day with code and numbers made him feel isolated. The large paycheck he received was no compensation for the tedious work he had to endure. The work simply went against the essence of who he was.

So, what excited my colleague? Interacting with people; selling and closing a deal; having the ability to control his destiny and income—the very opposite of his software job.

So many of us have the desire to change our lives and careers, but we allow our dreams to float off, like helium balloons. As the years go by, change simply seems too arduous. But once you commit yourself, anything is possible.

My colleague didn't quit his job, but he finally made a commitment to pursue his real passion. He began attending sales and product training. He read sales-related books, articles, and magazines. Even though he had good people skills, this didn't translate directly into sales prowess. He needed extensive practical experience, so he began working in the sales department with a small base and a high commission. This on-the-job training was invaluable in showing him the ropes and cuing him on aspects of sales that can only be learned by doing. He performed so well in this field that he eventually advanced to sales manager.

Commitment is a key component in learning; it creates the difference between wishing for something and attaining it.

Once you find your passion and commit to it, there will be no stopping you. You cannot learn enough.

I have carefully selected the following quotes and biographies of ten successful people who are committed lifelong learners.

LEARNING COMMMITMENT RELATED QUOTES

QUOTES AND BIOGRAPHIES OF SUCCESSFUL PEOPLE WHO ARE COMMITTED LIFELONG LEARNERS

ABRAHAM LINCOLN
(1809–1865)
16TH PRESIDENT OF THE UNITED STATES OF AMERICA

IT MAY be no exaggeration to claim that love of reading brought Abraham Lincoln to the White House. He estimated that his formal schooling had totaled to no more than a year, but his commitment to learn led him to borrow books and read whenever he could. It was necessity, he claimed, that led him to self-educate in order to fill the gaps in his knowledge. He taught himself math while working as a store clerk; surveying, when someone provided him the basic tools and a job; and law, when he was elected to the Illinois state legislature. He joined a local debate society to improve his public speaking.

His law partner said of Lincoln, "His ambition was a little engine that knew no rest." As the 16th president of the United States, Lincoln abolished slavery in the Confederacy and preserved the federal union. Despite being a man with little formal training, his speeches are studied as models of lofty eloquence.

I don't think much of a man who is not
wiser today than he was yesterday.

—Abraham Lincoln

Mahatma Gandhi
(1869–1948)
Political Activist & Partisan of Non-Violent Resistance

In his early life, Gandhi was unremarkable, an average student so painfully shy that he would become incapacitated when he had to speak in public. Despite his resentment of British control over India, he travelled to England in order to become a barrister. The years abroad were difficult for him, and he returned to India immediately after being accepted to the bar. Unable to make a living as a lawyer in India, he accepted a position in South Africa.

While there, he experienced even more repression than he had known in India under the British. The need for action overcame his timidity, and he became a committed advocate for the underclass of Indian immigrants in South Africa. After twenty years as an activist there, he brought his seasoned skills back to his Indian homeland and became one of the major actors in the struggle for Indian independence.

Live as if you were to die tomorrow.

Learn as if you were to live forever.

—Gandhi

LEONARDO DA VINCI
(1452–1519)
ARTIST AND RENAISSANCE MAN

LEONARDO WAS born in the Italian town of Vinci, near the culturally rich city of Florence. He was apprenticed as a youth to the master artist Andrea del Verrochio, but it was not long before the student had outpaced the master.

His insatiable desire for knowledge led him to so many diverse interests that Leonardo can be considered the model for the notion of a Renaissance man. His incomparable drawing ability was a way for him to record his scientific observations. Although known for painting the "Mona Lisa" and "The Last Supper," he did not complete many paintings in his lifetime. His nearly 2,500 drawings in notebooks offer a more complete picture of his wide-ranging interests and ideas. In the notebooks, he drew what he had observed and then described and explained the drawings in words, a forerunner to modern scientific drawing.

Learning never exhausts the mind.

—Leonardo da Vinci

CLAY P. BEDFORD
(1903–1991)
ENGINEER, INDUSTRIALIST, AND MANAGER

CLAY P. BEDFORD was a top executive of Kaiser Industries in California for nearly fifty years. During WWII, he oversaw the production of 727 ships in five years, a direct contribution to victory in the war. Bedford became known as an efficiency expert after he supervised construction of a WWII Liberty cargo ship in just four days and 15 minutes. He was later manager of a number of major projects, including the construction of the Central Highway in Cuba, and the Boulder, Grand Coulee, and Bonneville Dams.

During the Korean War, Bedford was summoned to Washington to assist with defense mobilization and production. Later in life, he was an advocate for the application of technology in the classroom.

You can teach a student a lesson for a day; but if you can teach him to learn by creating curiosity, he will continue the learning process as long as he lives.

—Clay P. Bedford

JOHN MACKEY
(b. 1953)
CEO, WHOLE FOODS MARKET

JOHN MACKEY split his college years between Trinity University and the University of Texas, taking only courses that interested him—mainly philosophy and religion, but no business classes. For a while he worked as a dishwasher and spent his nights reading in the library. He wasn't interested in vegetarianism, but he was committed to alternative lifestyles, so he moved into a vegetarian collective. He started to care about food and found a job in a health food store.

"I loved retail. I loved being around food. ... I loved the whole idea of it. And a thought entered into my mind that maybe this is what I could do."

Today, his Whole Foods chain has sales of 8 billion dollars per year. Mackey thinks of himself as a capitalist do-gooder.

"The more money we make, the more good we can do, " he says.

My philosophy is that life is all about learning and growing, and that life can be a real adventure of learning, growing, compassion, and joyfulness.

—John Mackey

YOGI BERRA
(b. 1925)
AMERICAN MAJOR LEAGUE BASEBALL PLAYER AND MANAGER

YOGI BERRA is considered one of baseball's greatest catchers and clutch hitters. He was among the New York Yankee's most feared hitters at a time when they were virtually unbeatable, leading the team in Runs Batted In (RBIs) for five straight years. He won ten major league championships and three Most Valuable Player awards. He caught Don Larsen's famous no-hitter in the 1956 World Series. Elected to the Baseball Hall of Fame in 1972, he has since been a successful manager.

Berra has been committed to youth organizations and education throughout his career, while admitting he himself wasn't a good student.

He is known for his colorful use of the language, coining such phrases as, "The future ain't what it used to be;" "It ain't over 'til it's over;" and "When you come to a fork in the road ... take it."

Life is a learning experience, only if you learn.

—Yogi Berra

GEORGE CARLIN
(1937–2008)
COMEDIAN

GEORGE CARLIN was in show business for over fifty years. He started out as a radio disk jockey and moved to stand-up as part of the short-lived comedy team of (Jack) Burns and Carlin. As a comedian, he attained notoriety with his "Seven Dirty Words" routine in which he mentioned that there were seven words that you couldn't ever say over the airwaves, and then went on to say them—repeatedly. He, the routine, and the words were the focus of a 1978 U.S. Supreme Court case, F.C.C. v. Pacifica Foundation. A 5-4 decision by the court affirmed the government's authority to regulate indecent material on public airwaves.

Carlin went on to many media appearances. He was the first host for Saturday Night Live, won five Grammys, wrote books, and acted on television and in movies. Just a week before Carlin's unexpected death, he was named the 2008 winner of the Kennedy Center Mark Twain Prize for American humor.

Keep learning. Learn more about the computer, crafts, gardening, whatever. Never let the brain idle.

—George Carlin

ROBERT MAYNARD HUTCHINS
(1899–1977)

U.S. EDUCATIONAL PHILOSOPHER; PRESIDENT OF THE UNIVERSITY OF CHICAGO

SON OF AN OBERLIN COLLEGE FACULTY MEMBER, Robert Hutchins recalled, "Our recreations were principally two: reading and physical exercise." Since he didn't much care for sports, he read all the more.

Hutchins graduated from Yale Law School and became its Dean while still in his 20s. He gained national renown through his work in introducing the findings of psychology, sociology, and logic within the rules of evidence. He was named President of the University of Chicago at the age of thirty and remained at the university for the next twenty years. Hutchins supported broad liberal studies for the first two years of college and, with Mortimer Adler, introduced the Great Books program.

Hutchins finally left the university to become head of the newly formed Ford Foundation, where he founded the Fund for Adult Education.

The objective of education is to prepare the young to educate themselves throughout their lives.

—Robert Maynard Hutchins

JOHN H. JOHNSON
(1918–2005)
PUBLISHER

JOHN H. JOHNSON'S Arkansas hometown didn't have a Black high school, but he was so committed to his education that he repeated 8th grade just to continue learning. His mother expected great things of him. She worked for years under harsh conditions to raise money for a move to Chicago so that her son could go to high school. He not only finished high school, he went on to take classes part-time at the University of Chicago and Northwestern University while working at an insurance company. A few years later, he founded Ebony Magazine, and still later, Jet. He is acknowledged as the first entrepreneur to recognize the buying power of the Black population.

Johnson believed that hard work and perseverance would open any door. Although he began in poverty, he became the first African-American to appear on the Forbes list of 400 wealthiest Americans.

What a relief it was to discover that
I wasn't really an idiot! I simply had
a learning disability.

—John H. Johnson

Mortimer Adler
(1902–2001)
American Philosopher, Educator, and Author

ADLER'S GREAT delight was in bringing knowledge to ordinary men and women. Although he was an excellent student, he dropped out of school at the age of fourteen to become a newspaper copy boy. His original intention was to become a journalist, but when he read Plato, he opted for philosophy instead. He attended Columbia University on a scholarship and eventually earned a Ph.D. in Psychology. He then taught at the University of Chicago for twenty years.

In 1943, Adler came up with the idea of compiling the *Great Books of the Western World*. He was associate editor of the project, which was first published in 1952 by the Encyclopaedia Britannica and the University of Chicago and consisted of 54 volumes. He believed these works should be part of everyone's education. For a time, they comprised a canon for Western literature.

The purpose of learning is growth,
and our minds, unlike our bodies, can
continue growing as long as we live.

—Mortimer Adler

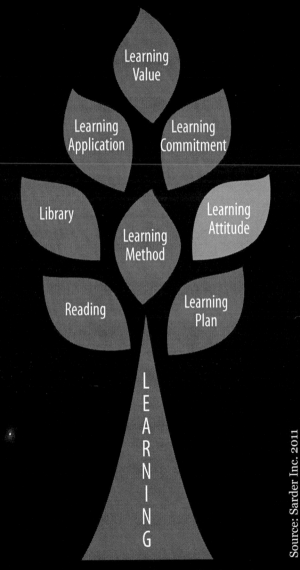

Learning Value

Learning Application

Learning Commitment

Library

Learning Method

Learning Attitude

Reading

Learning Plan

L E A R N I N G

Source: Sarder Inc. 2011

Steps to becoming a passionate lifelong learner

LEARNING ATTITUDE

Develop the Right Attitude to Continuous Learning.

I award a Sarder Scholarship monthly to an ambitious individual who wishes to begin or advance an IT career. The scholarship provides $2,500 towards any public or online classes at NetCom.

The Sarder Scholarship was created to give back to the community and spread our culture of lifelong learning. We believe that learning should be a never- ending process, as it alone fuels personal growth. We are honored to contribute to our students' growth every day.

One of the most memorable winners is Caroline Christie, a teacher in her 60s, who works in a school for gifted boys. She teaches computers to the boys and also supports the school staff with their software needs. She applied for the scholarship because she wanted to upgrade her web development skills and remain current in her field, but didn't have the funds to continue this education on her own.

At an age when others are winding down their careers or fantasizing about retirement options, Christie's attitude is one of continued growth and commitment to those she teaches—especially underprivileged boys, who would never have a chance without her dedication.

Whenever we challenge ourselves with new learning, we remain healthier and happier, and discover that we possess far more potential than we know.

It's never too late to learn.

After many years of observing students, I believe there are three types of learners:

The "Don't Care" Learner: The "Don't Care" learner possesses little curiosity about the world; the status quo is perfectly fine with her. She prefers passive activities, such as watching television and playing computer games. She dislikes reading and will only attend seminars or courses when forced by a job requirement. Even then she drags her feet. Once at a seminar she fidgets, sighs, and checks her phone. She may be physically present, but mentally she is far away.

The "Know it All" Learner: This type of learner already believes he knows everything. He acts as if having a college degree means he doesn't need to learn anything more. He's the first to declare his expertise, even when he only has the most rudimentary knowledge. Of all learners, he knows the least because he's stopped growing.

The "Don't Know Enough" Learner: This is a person who, like Caroline Christie, is actively learning throughout her life, who always has a book by her side, a goal in her mind, a new idea that she is considering. These learners seem more alive, because they are open to all topics and are interested in whatever new knowledge they encounter. They are not hemmed in by one field. They know that embracing the infinite possibilities of knowledge is the key to success. Embracing a pro-learning attitude makes all the difference in what you make of your life. The choice is yours .

I have carefully selected the following quotes and biographies of eight successful people with the right learning attitude.

LEARNING ATTITUDE RELATED QUOTES

Quotes and Biographies of Successful People With the Right Learning Attitude

DONALD TRUMP
(b.1946)
AMERICAN BUSINESS MAGNATE & CEO OF THE TRUMP ORGANIZATION

DONALD TRUMP has made it a point to learn from the masters. During business school, he found himself drawn to the best thinkers and achievers in history, from politics to the arts, from science to literature.

His approach is to draw on great historical figures, not just for perspective but also for inspiration. He has read biographies of Churchill, Lincoln, Picasso, Einstein, and many other renowned thinkers.

After joining his father's real estate company, Trump branched out on his own. He has become a cultural fixture with his own television show and continuing real estate projects. He also sells his own bottled water, apparel, and vodka, and has authored several books, making his estimated worth $3 billion, according to Forbes in 2010.

You can't know it all. No matter how smart you are, no matter how comprehensive your education, no matter how wide ranging your experience, there is simply no way to acquire all the wisdom you need to make your business thrive.

—Donald Trump

Albert Schweitzer
(1875–1965)
Nobel Peace Prize Winner

ALBERT SCHWEITZER'S approach toward learning was nurtured by his childhood environment. He was born in Alsace, a disputed region that at the time was part of Germany. His father was the local Protestant pastor. Two different congregations—Lutheran Evangelical and Catholic—shared the church where he preached. Growing up in such an accepting climate fostered in young Albert a tolerance that made him open-minded in his approach to learning. This attitude would serve him throughout his life. He promoted a universal Christian spirit of unity and a reverence for life.

At the age of 30, he entered a life of service to others. In practical terms, this meant that he charted a new career course: he left his position as a successful theologian and entered medical school. His humanitarian efforts as a physician in Africa captured the imagination of the world and won him the Nobel Peace Prize in 1952.

As we acquire more knowledge, things do not become more comprehensible, but more mysterious.

—Albert Schweitzer

"Og" Mandino
(1923–1996)
American Author

"...My loving mother...had a special dream for her son. 'Someday,' she would tell me, again and again, 'someday you will be a writer...'"

But when Og's mother died almost immediately after high school graduation, his plans for college were put on the back burner. He became a bombardier in WWII and flew 30 missions over Germany. After the war, he was uncertain what direction to take and sunk into debt and alcoholism.

He felt he had reached the end of his line when one day he wandered out of the cold weather into a library. He pulled some self-help books from the shelves and began reading. His luck began to turn, and he returned to his dream of writing, authoring a self-help book called *The Greatest Salesman in the World*. It received an endorsement from a co-founder of Amway, Corp., and sales skyrocketed. He continued to write many other bestsellers about success.

Take the attitude of a student, never be too big to ask questions, never know too much to learn something new.

—Og Mandino

OSCAR WILDE
(1854–1900)
PLAYWRIGHT

OSCAR WILDE had a somewhat privileged upbringing. His father was a leading eye and ear surgeon who also wrote books, while his mother was an ardent Irish nationalist who wrote poetry. He was taught French and German at home at a young age. Later, he excelled in the study of Classics at Trinity College, Dublin, and Oxford University.

Wilde made a name for himself largely by being an outrageous wit whose company was much sought after in Victorian London. He supported himself by giving lectures on culture and writing. For a time, he was editor of a women's magazine. Wilde's best-known works are probably *The Picture of Dorian Gray* and his play *The Importance of Being Earnest*.

I am not young enough to know everything.

—Oscar Wilde

WINSTON CHURCHILL
(1874–1965)
STATESMAN & WINNER OF NOBEL PRIZE IN LITERATURE

WINSTON CHURCHILL was the son of a British lord and an American heiress. He graduated with honors from the Royal Military College and then saw action in Cuba, India, Egypt, Sudan, and the front lines of World War I. First achieving prominence as a war correspondent, he wrote five books by the age of 26. He became a national hero in Great Britain when he escaped from a Boer prison during the Boer War.

Churchill was elected to Parliament at the age of 25, and served for the next 60 years, most notably as Prime Minister and Minister of Defense. He won the Nobel Prize for Literature in 1953, having written a large number of histories, including his memoirs of WWII in six volumes. One biographer suggested that the reason Churchill wrote so many books was so that he could continue his education throughout his lifetime.

Churchill inspired England with fortitude through one of its darkest periods during World War II, largely through the force of his own character.

I am always ready to learn, although I do not always like being taught.

—Winston Churchill

SOCRATES
(469–399)
GREEK PHILOSOPHER

VERY LITTLE reliable information exists about Socrates and his life because he wrote no books. What we know about him comes chiefly from the writings of others, especially his student Plato. Socrates' contemporaries feared that he was corrupting their youth with dangerous ideas. His questioning method for arriving at the truth seemed to erode secure beliefs of the day. Socrates's questioning of his pupils often led them to reevaluate their parents' beliefs.

"The unexamined life is not worth living for a human being," Socrates insisted (Plato, *Apology* 38a).

In the end, Socrates was executed for irreverence to the gods.

As for me, all I know is that
I know nothing.

—Socrates

HENRY L. DOHERTY
(1870–1939)
UTILITIES PIONEER

HENRY DOHERTY grew up poor and left school to become an office boy for the gas company at the age of 12. Fortunately for him, he had a strong work ethic and a plan for self-education. Within eight years he had worked his way up to chief engineer. Then he began acquiring utility assets. At the time of his death he was worth an estimated $200 million, and the utility holding company that he had founded held over one billion dollars in assets. That company was later known as CITGO Petroleum.

Doherty was a key figure in developing the gas and electrical utilities industries in the U.S. He envisioned the potential of providing utilities for the midwest's growing cities. His company was involved in virtually every oil and gas discovery in Oklahoma for forty years, and he created a research company to train petroleum geologists and engineers.

Get over the idea that only children should spend their time in study. Be a student so long as you still have something to learn, and this will mean all your life.

—Henry L. Doherty

VERNON HOWARD
(1918–1992)
AMERICAN SPIRITUAL TEACHER, AUTHOR, AND PHILOSOPHER

VERNON HOWARD graduated high school but took college classes only intermittently. He was, nevertheless, widely read, claiming in his later years to have read everything from the New Testament to Kant to Zen Buddhism. He taught himself to be a professional writer, beginning with magazine filler, humor, and children's craft books before turning to self-improvement.

"Finally I just got fed up and decided to figure out what life what all about," he wrote. He authored a large number of self-help books expressing his philosophy, borrowing from different spiritual traditions and presenting his insights in clear language suited for a modern audience. His central message was that the way to escape human suffering was to identify the negative in oneself and leave it behind. In 1979, he founded the New Life Church and Literary Foundation in Boulder City, Nevada, as a focal point for his ideas.

Always walk through life as if you have something new to learn and you will.

—Vernon Howard

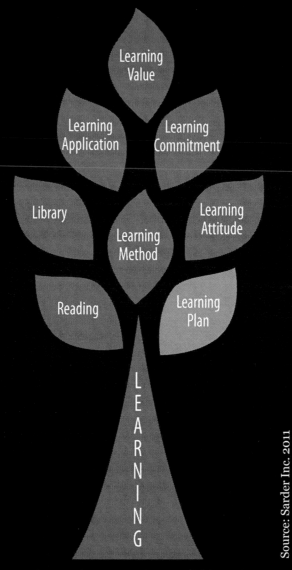

Learning Value

Learning Application

Learning Commitment

Library

Learning Method

Learning Attitude

Reading

Learning Plan

LEARNING

Steps to becoming a passionate lifelong learner

Source: Sarder Inc. 2011

Step 4.
Learning Plan

Develop an Effective Learning
Plan to Excel in Your Field.

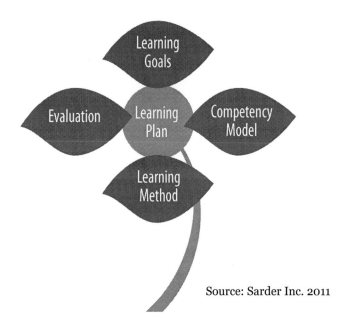

Source: Sarder Inc. 2011

When I founded NetCom Learning in 1997 right out of college, I knew that I was taking a risk. I wasn't choosing a secure job with an established organization, but one that in the beginning was simply me and my dream. I didn't even have a degree in business, but in computer science. I knew that I would have to learn everything it took to make this business successful. And I had to set up a learning plan in order for my business to survive, let alone thrive.

I found that the fantasies I'd had of being my own boss, reporting to work whenever I felt like it, and gaining wealth quickly were naïve.

Continuous learning, knowledge, and dedicated commitment were my formula for success.

Throughout my career, I have benefited greatly from having a learning plan in place at all times, one that consists of four basic components:

Learning Goals: Have specific goals and allow flexibility for them to change when necessary.

In the initial stage of my business, my learning goals were focused on becoming a business expert and a successful CEO.

Competency Model: Acquire the necessary knowledge, skills, and attributes for all aspects of success, whatever your business or career.

In my case, I asked myself, what are the different domains that I need to master in order to achieve my goals? I realized that I needed to learn about sales, marketing, business development, people management, people development, accounting, finance, basic corporate law, management, and strategy. I also needed to improve my presentation, communication, and interpersonal skills.

Learning Methods: Consider the five learning methods, and find a way to incorporate them into your learning plan.

In the early years of my business, I applied all five types of learning methods—self study, coaching, mentoring, on the job training, and classroom study. And just as importantly, I'm still using these learning methods to attain new skills.

Evaluation: Every learning plan should be evaluated to determine success.

When my business had grown from $0 to $10M revenue, I re-evaluated my goals and began to shift my focus away from day-to-day operations.

As my role changed, I knew it was essential to change my behavior. Using the same learning plan basics, I began developing my leadership skills. Later, as the organization grew even larger, I shifted to a learning plan geared toward increasing value through growth, profit, and trust.

The beauty of a learning plan is that it can be changed as you and your business develop and evolve; you simply tailor it to wherever you are.

"He Who Fails to Plan, Plans to Fail" is a proverb as true today as ever.

I have carefully selected the following quotes and biographies of ten successful people who have developed effective learning plans to excel in their fields.

Learning Plan related Quotes

Quotes and Biographies of Successful People who Have Developed Effective Learning Plans to Excel in Their Fields

PETER DRUCKER
(1909–2005)
AUTHOR & MANAGEMENT CONSULTANT

REGARDED AS THE FATHER of modern management, Peter Drucker was a proponent of learning as a lifelong process for keeping abreast of change; in fact, he cultivated the habit of studying something new every three or four years. He valued education, business accountability, and personal responsibility to society. During his long consulting career, Drucker's clients included many large corporations, such as General Electric, Coca-Cola, Citicorp, IBM, and Intel. With these companies, he helped create the foundations of modern management.

Drucker foresaw and helped shape a number of important developments in economics and management, from decentralization and privatization to the emergence of our information-based society. He published over 30 books, and was awarded the Presidential Medal of Freedom in 2002 by President George W. Bush in recognition for his work in the field of management.

Plans are only good intentions unless they immediately degenerate into actions.

—Peter Drucker

BRIAN TRACY
(b.1944)
BEST-SELLING WRITER & MOTIVATIONAL SPEAKER

THE HUMAN MIND, Brian Tracy reminds us, has an almost infinite potential for learning and processing information. To access this incredible resource, Tracy has formulated techniques for accelerating learning and retaining information.

His methods have helped countless individuals achieve their personal and business goals. He has consulted with more than 1,000 companies and addressed more than 4,000,000 people in talks and seminars worldwide. He has also written and produced many audio and video learning programs, including his bestselling *Psychology of Achievement*. He recently launched Brian Tracy University to help entrepreneurs, business owners, and sales professionals.

A clear vision, backed by definite plans, gives you a tremendous feeling of confidence and personal power.

—Brian Tracy

Andrew Carnegie
(1835–1919)
Industrialist, Entrepreneur, and Philanthropist

ANDREW CARNEGIE came from a family of social reformers who believed that the rich had a moral obligation to distribute their wealth for the public good. Carnegie did not forget this when he became wealthy.

At the age of 13, however,. he was a poor factory worker in Pennsylvania. He received an education largely through the generosity of a local resident, who opened his private library to working boys. Young Carnegie made very active use of this library. Over time, he worked his way up a series of jobs until he rose to superintendent of the Pennsylvania Railroad and eventually formed the first of his many companies. He sold his Carnegie Steel Company to J.P. Morgan, who merged it with other companies to create U.S. Steel.

Carnegie used his fortune to found the Carnegie Corporation of New York, the Carnegie Endowment for International Peace, Carnegie Mellon University, and Carnegie Hall.

A man's reading program should be as carefully planned as his daily diet, for that too is food, without which he cannot grow mentally.

—Andrew Carnegie

Confucius
(551 BC–479 BC)
Teacher & Philosopher

Individuals, taught Confucius, are responsible for their actions, behavior, and accomplishments, even though some things are beyond their control.

Confucius had a good deal to say about leadership that still rings true today. Moral education, he believed, is vital for teaching people in leadership positions how to live up to their responsibilities. Leaders should always demonstrate virtue to the people under them. Moral authority would allow a ruler to maintain order without the use of force. If a leader leads by use of virtue, subordinates will be influenced by the ruler's values and also display those virtues themselves.

Knowledge was also central to Confucius. He believed that without serious study of a subject, a person could not claim knowledge of it. Confucius' book of teachings, *Analects*, was the model for behavior used by Chinese government officials for over two thousand years.

A man who does not plan long ahead will find trouble at his door.

—Confucius

GEORGE S. PATTON, JR.
(1884–1945)
MILITARY GENERAL

PATTON'S PARENTS read to him as a child, nurturing a love of reading that took root despite his probable dyslexia. He came from a military family and from his earliest years wanted to be a soldier. He developed a lifelong pattern of study that combined focused reading with on-the-job military training.

With WWI blazing in Europe, Patton was asked to create an American tank school in France. He observed the French use of tanks, spoke with French and British tank commanders, and learned how to drive a tank. When the US created its own tank corps in 1917, Patton was its first member.

During WWII, the Third Army, with Patton in command, swept across Europe using Patton's study of the Norman Conquest to guide his own invasion of France. He is considered one of the most successful field commanders in American military history.

A good plan, violently executed now, is better than a perfect plan next week.

—George S. Patton

Alan Lakein
Effectiveness Expert

LAKEIN CALLED himself a Time Planning and Life Goals consultant. In his book, *How to Get Control Of Your Time and Your Life,* Lakein claimed he knew his time management system worked because it had given him control over his own life. A graduate of Johns Hopkins University with a Harvard MBA, Lakein had started out as a computer programmer but moved into management consulting. He admitted learning from other authorities, like Peter Drucker, but he developed his own system that he felt was more effective. As a result, he founded his own consulting company, the first full-time, time management company. His clients ranged from famous individuals like Gloria Steinem to corporate clients like Bank of America and IBM.

Lakein's advice to clients usually began with a question, one that he often asked himself: "What is the most effective use of your time right now?" To answer his question, he advised, you must establish priorities, goals, and a concrete plan of action.

Planning is bringing the future into the present so that you can do something about it now.

—Alan Lakein

Lester Robert Bittel
(1918–2003)
Authority on Management & Supervision

Lester Bittel's degree was in Industrial Engineering, but his career was dedicated to improving the competence and professionalism of workers and managers. He accomplished this as a training manager, a professor at James Madison University, as the director of several trade journals at McGraw-Hill, and as the author of approximately 50 books.

His book, *What Every Supervisor Should Know*, is the standard text on management and is used internationally by colleges and corporations alike. Bittel wrote the book in order to provide a learning plan for workers and supervisors. He wanted to provide practical information for use on the job, but he also wanted the material to be enjoyable and simple to learn. His book includes clear learning objectives and offers advice on how to improve personal job performance in order to prepare for advancement.

Good plans shape good decisions. That's why good planning helps to make elusive dreams come true.

—Lester Robert Bittel

ELEANOR ROOSEVELT
(1884–1962)
FIRST LADY & SOCIAL ACTIVIST

GROWING UP, Eleanor Roosevelt was first introduced to progressive ideas at a boarding school, through her teacher and mentor, Marie Souvestre. Souvestre took Eleanor as her personal traveling companion throughout Europe, where Eleanor witnessed the lives of the poor and working class.

As FDR's First Lady, Roosevelt was known as a humanitarian. Social causes were her interest; political ones, her husband's. Yet Eleanor advanced from being politically naïve to holding weekly meetings with female reporters, asking them to educate the public, particularly women, on important political issues. As a key member of the U.N. Commission on Human Rights, she considered her work to create and promote the "Universal Declaration of Human Rights" to be her most important legacy. At the time of her death, Adlai Stevenson eulogized her by saying, "She would rather light a candle than curse the darkness, and her glow has warmed the world."

It takes as much energy to wish as it does to plan.

—Eleanor Roosevelt

ZIG ZIGLAR
(b. 1926)
MOTIVATIONAL SPEAKER, AUTHOR

FOR DECADES, Zig Ziglar has been motivating others. He began his sales career as a first grader selling peanuts for six cents a bag on the streets of Yazoo City, Mississippi. He said it was then he began connecting with people. He later served in the Navy and attended the University of South Carolina. He worked as a top salesman in different companies for twenty years until becoming interested in motivational speaking. His approach has been influenced by his Christian faith.

Ziglar has published over 40 books and is an active supporter of the Boy Scouts of America, which awarded him the Silver Buffalo Award in 2001. Two supporters whose lives were positively changed by him created the Zig Ziglar Center for Ethical Leadership at Southern Nazarene University.

The Ziglar Corporation is based in Dallas and continues Ziglar's corporate training and personal development work under the direction of his son and son-in-law.

You need a plan to build a house. To build a life, it is even more important to have a plan or goal.

—Zig Ziglar

NAPOLEON HILL
(1883–1970)
AMERICAN AUTHOR

HILL WAS one of the earliest American authors to write books on achieving personal success through positive thinking, coining the expression, "What the mind of man can conceive and believe, it can achieve."

Hill was a reporter, writing a series of stories on the rich and powerful, when his interview with steel magnate Andrew Carnegie took an unexpected turn—one that would change the course of Hill's life. Carnegie suggested to him that there was a simple formula for success that anyone could understand and achieve. He challenged Hill to interview 500 successful men and test whether such a formula really existed. Hill rose to the challenge, interviewing the most important and influential people of the time, including Thomas Edison, John D. Rockefeller, and Henry Ford. A series of motivational books and training courses followed, including the ever-popular *Think and Grow Rich*.

Reduce your plan to writing. The moment you complete this, you will have definitely given concrete form to the intangible desire.

—Napoleon Hill

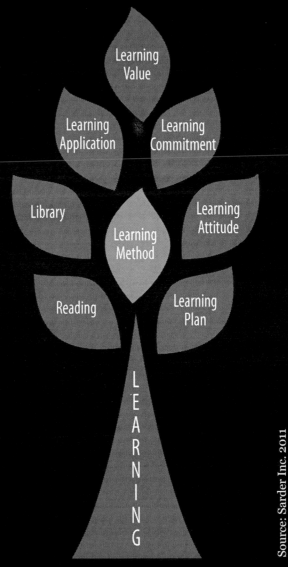

Learning Value

Learning Application

Learning Commitment

Library

Learning Method

Learning Attitude

Reading

Learning Plan

LEARNING

Source: Sarder Inc. 2011

Steps to becoming a passionate lifelong learner

LEARNING METHODS

Become an Effective Learner by Combining a Variety of Learning Methods.

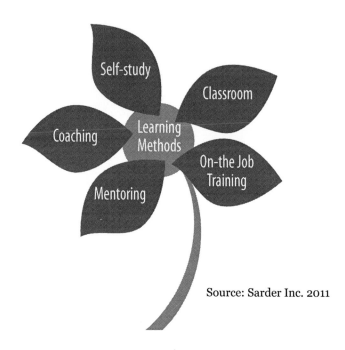

Source: Sarder Inc. 2011

It's not easy to reach your destination without using proven methods that will help guide you there. The most effective way to reach your goals is to develop your own learning method. This will lend your learning enjoyment and ease.

There are five effective learning methods. Once you understand them, you can mix and match to create a blend that is just right for you.

LEARNING METHODS

Coaching: In my own life I've used many coaches, but my father was the main one, the original person who motivated me to perform at my personal best, who inspired and energized me. Coaches can help in all areas of business performance, from leadership and team playing to sales.

Mentoring: A mentor is typically a person who has experience in your industry or profession and gives you guidance targeted toward your specific needs. In my own case, I have regular meetings with other CEOs, where we mentor each other by asking questions and sharing experiences.

Self-Study: There are many forms of self-study, including reading, self-paced e-learning, audio and video learning, and webinars. Reading is my own favorite type of self-study, and I've found that it has a powerful effect on my brain. Each book teaches me something valuable about myself and my business.

Classroom: The most formal of learning methods, classroom learning can take place in both online and physical classrooms. In our company's case, we utilize a combination approach, virtual by nature, but attended in real time by students throughout the country, who can collaborate with each other.

On-the-Job: This is a system of apprenticeship in which one person shows another how a particular task is performed or watches him carry out a task to make sure he's doing it correctly. I have used this system throughout my career, learning from clients, vendors, instructors, my leadership team, and employees.

Most successful learners combine all five of these techniques in some way. Finding your ideal method will encourage the habits that promote lifelong learning.

It was essential for NetCom Learning to promote a learning environment that reached out to every employee. Using these five main learning methods was the best way to ensure that every employee had a path to follow. There is no employee who is left out of this process, because every employee is valuable to NetCom Learning. The result of this strategic implementation was a 20% growth in productivity. This happened because we found ways to stimulate each employee's learning method without adding unnecessary manpower. The value of utilizing my employees' brilliant mind power has been a great motivator for NetCom Learning to continue our daily pursuit of business and personal excellence.

If you'd like to find out more about the specific techniques that I have found highly effective, I encourage you to read my book Effective Learning Methods: How Do You Develop the Most Effective Learning Method?

Map out your learning methods ahead of time, and head for success.

I have carefully selected the following quotes and biographies of of eleven successful people who have become effective learners by combining a variety of learning methods.

Learning Method-Related Quotes

Quotes and biographies of successful people who have become effective learners by combining a variety of learning methods.

Jack Welch

(b.1935)

Business Writer & Former Chairman/CEO, General Electric

ONE OF THE HALLMARKS of Jack Welch's success has been linking learning with action. This, he believes, gives an organization the ultimate competitive advantage.

Welch joined GE as a chemical engineer for its plastics division in Pittsfield, Massachusetts, and was named the company's youngest Vice President in 1972. In April, 1981, he became its 8th Chairman and CEO.

From 1981-2001, Welch served as GE's Chairman and Chief Executive Officer. GE saw tremendous growth under his management, from a market value of $14 billion to one of $410 billion by the time of his departure. In 1999, Fortune named him the "Manager of the Century," and the *Financial Times* recently named him one of the three most-admired business leaders in the world today.

I've learned that mistakes can often be as good a teacher as success.

—Jack Welch

BILL GATES
(b.1955)
AMERICAN BUSINESS MAGNATE & FOUNDER AND CHAIRMAN, MICROSOFT

BILL GATES has become a worldwide icon. Raised in Seattle, he attended Harvard after high school. Gates took a leave of absence from Harvard when the opportunity arose to create his own company—Microsoft, where he would later launch the operating system, Windows.

Gates believes in constantly learning new things: "I... place a high value on having a passion for ongoing learning. When I was pretty young, I picked up the habit of reading lots of books."

In 2010, Gates' worth was estimated in excess of $53 billion. The Bill & Melinda Gates Foundation, which he established with his wife, is dedicated to bringing innovations in health, development, and learning to the global community.

We all learn best in our own ways. Some people do better studying one subject at a time, while some do better studying three things at once. Some people do best studying in a structured, linear way, while others do best jumping around, 'surrounding' a subject.

—Bill Gates

OPRAH WINFREY
(b.1954)
MEDIA ICON & PHILANTHROPIST

BORN IN MISSISSIPPI, Oprah Winfrey started her career as co-anchor for a radio station. Today she has her own television channel, magazine, and website. She is often cited as the richest African-American of the 20th century, with an estimated worth of $2.3 billion in 2010.

A long-time believer in the power of learning, Winfrey dreamed of building a first-class school to nurture, educate, and transform gifted South African girls from impoverished backgrounds into the country's future leaders. Her dream became a reality in 2007, when the Oprah Winfrey Leadership Academy for Girls–South Africa opened its doors.

She has said, "For everyone who succeeds, it's because there's somebody there to show you the way out."

What I know for sure is that behind every catastrophe, there are great lessons to be learned.

—Oprah Winfrey

PATRICK WHITE
(1912–1990)
NOVELIST & WINNER OF NOBEL PRIZE IN LITERATURE

AUTHOR PATRICK WHITE suffered from severe asthma as a child and spent his early school years separated from his family, who sent him to healthier locations. He credited his asthma for his early interest in reading and writing.

Before university, he attempted to find a home on the land by working as a stockman on his uncle's sheep station. He learned that "the talk was endlessly of wool and weather," so he headed to Cambridge for more intellectual pursuits. There he studied French and German literature and traveled abroad to improve his grasp of the languages. Upon graduation, his puzzled father nevertheless agreed to modestly support White while he began a writing career.

White wrote a number of novels, short stories, and plays, and in 1973 was the first Australian to be awarded the Nobel Prize for Literature.

I forget what I was taught. I only remember what I have learnt.

—Patrick White

ARISTOTLE
(384 BC–322 BC)
GREEK PHILOSOPHER

ARISTOTLE WAS trained in medicine before being sent to Athens to study philosophy under Plato, student of Socrates. After Plato's death, he left Athens and traveled, eventually going to Macedonia to tutor the man who would later conquer an empire, Alexander the Great.

Upon his return to Athens, Aristotle set up his own school and taught in much the same way as Plato had before him. Aristotle left a lasting impact on history. His philosophy was the basis for much of medieval thought, and he inspired major medieval thinkers in all three great Western religions: Thomas Aquinas in Christianity, Averroes (ibn Rashd) in Islam, and Maimonides in Judaism.

What we have to learn to do, we learn by doing.

—Aristotle

MARK TWAIN
(1835–1910)
AMERICAN WRITER

MARK TWAIN was the pen name of Samuel Langhorne Clemens, who was a firm believer in lifelong learning; in his book *The Prince and the Pauper*, he wrote: "Learning softeneth the heart and breedeth gentleness and charity...."

In 1862, Twain began work as a reporter for the Virginia City Territorial Enterprise, where he created news stories, editorials, and sketches. He became a well-known and well-loved storyteller, with novels such as *The Adventures of Tom Sawyer* and *The Adventures of Huckleberry Finn*. Twain's later years were filled with public honors, including degrees from Oxford and Yale. Probably the most famous American of the late 19th century, he was a celebrity wherever he went. Today, his legacy lives on in the books he published.

I have never let my schooling interfere with my education.

—Mark Twain

Jim Rohn
(1930–2009)
Motivational Speaker

Jim Rohn authored a great many motivational books and audio–video programs. He grew up on a farm in Idaho, the only son of a minister and his wife. He attended college for one year, but quit to get a job and help his family. After a few years, he realized his life was going nowhere, but that he lacked the vision and skills to give it direction.

Then he met Earl Shoaff, a motivational speaker and direct-marketing vitamin salesman. He went to work for Shoaff, and under his guidance, Rohn embarked on a path of personal development. Sometime after Shoaff's early death at age 49, Rohn gave a talk at the local Rotary Club, which he entitled, "Idaho Farm Boy Makes It to Beverly Hills," which turned out to be the start of his career as a motivational speaker. At the time of his death, he had been a motivational speaker for 43 years. Many in the personal development business count Jim Rohn as their mentor.

Formal education will make you a living; self-education will make you a fortune.

—Jim Rohn

LLOYD ALEXANDER
(1924–2007)
AUTHOR OF JUVENILE FICTION

LLOYD ALEXANDER'S parents did not like to read books, but he did. He liked reading so well, in fact, that by the age of 15 he had decided he wanted to be a writer. His parents were alarmed and insisted he do something useful. They got him a job as a bank messenger; he used the experience to write his first book.

Alexander recalled, "Shakespeare, Dickens, Mark Twain, and so many others were my dearest friends and greatest teachers. I loved all the world's mythologies..."

His writing was influenced by the mythology he loved to read. A stint in Wales during army service brought Welsh mythology to his attention, and he drew upon it for his award-winning series, *The Chronicles of Prydain*. Most of Alexander's books are fantasy, and they provided him a way to write about real social injustice. He wrote more than 40 books and won a number of awards, including the National Book Award and the Newberry Medal for children's literature.

We learn more by looking for the answer to a question and not finding it than we do from learning the answer itself.

—Lloyd Alexander

MALCOLM GLADWELL
(b.1963)
BEST-SELLING AUTHOR

MALCOLM GLADWELL began reading on his sixth birthday, and four months later could read anything, including the Bible. Growing up, he says, "I would always come to the university ... and I'd often go into the library. ... The idea that there was a place with thousands and thousands of books—ten times bigger than the [local] library ... —was wonderful for me."

His bestselling book, *Outliers: The Story of Success,* investigates why some people are successful, while others never realize their potential. He concludes that successful people are the result of many factors and interactions in their environment, a mix of opportunity and chance. According to him, almost every successful individual or organization puts in at least 10,000 hours of practice first, which averages out to about four hours per day for ten years.

Gladwell's other bestsellers include *The Tipping Point.* He is a staff writer for *The New Yorker.*

We learn by example and by direct experience because there are real limits to the adequacy of verbal instruction.

—Malcolm Gladwell

Lou Holtz

(b.1937)

American Football Coach

Lou Holtz has had a succession of successful careers. He coached college football teams in six different college programs, frequently leading his teams to bowl games and top-20 rankings. After coaching, he became a sportscaster before being elected to the College Football Hall of Fame in 2008. He subsequently became known as a motivational speaker.

Holtz only reads motivational books geared toward self-improvement. He believes in writing a life philosophy that can be supplemented or edited over time. In it, he suggests, the following questions should be answered: What do you believe? What do you stand for? What are the things you value? What are you willing to die for? What will you tolerate? What won't you tolerate? What kind of parent do you want to be?

"You add to it, but at least you have a basic philosophy to live by," he says.

I never learn anything talking. I only learn things when I ask questions.

—Lou Holtz

Marvin Minsky
(b.1927)
American Scientist

MARVIN LEE MINSKY is a pioneer in the field of Artificial Intelligence. He earned his BA from Harvard and PhD from Princeton; both degrees were in Mathematics. In 1958, Minsky joined the faculty of MIT, where he has remained ever since. The following year, he and a colleague founded the MIT Artificial Intelligence Project.

Minsky was an adviser on the movie 2001: A Space Odyssey and is referred to in the movie and book. In 1989, he moved to MIT's media laboratory, where he became Toshiba Professor of Media Arts and Sciences. He is concurrently Professor of Electrical Engineering and Computer Science. Minsky built the first neural network simulator in 1951. He designed some of the first visual scanners, and his other inventions include robotic arms and hands. He is currently working on giving machines the ability to reason like humans.

You don't understand anything until you learn it more than one way.

—Marvin Minsky

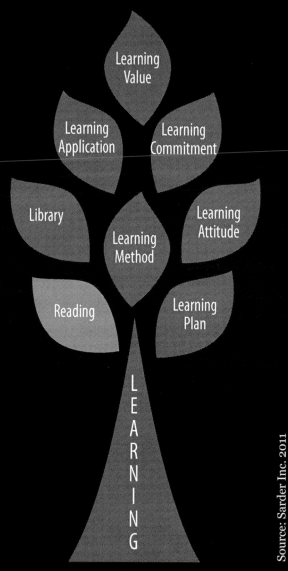

Steps to becoming a passionate lifelong learner

Source: Sarder Inc. 2011

STEP 6.
READING

Read an Hour Each Day and
Grow Wealthy.

One of my life goals is to encourage a new and vibrant learning culture. The easiest, most satisfying way to learn is by reading. Reading only an hour a day can significantly change your life. Try committing to this for the next three months. You'll find great inspiration. Your brain will start to change and so will your life.

When you walk into most American living rooms, you're more likely to find a flat-screened TV rather than a bookcase full of volumes. These televisions don't just take up walls, but also minds.

Statistics about American reading habits are shocking. The American Bookseller Association states that only 42% of college graduates read even one book after they leave school. Furthermore, only 30% of Americans have visited a bookstore in the past five years.

But in China and India, this is not the case. They are not spending their days in front of television. They're studying, reading, and learning. And the results are clear.

My father was my role model in reading; throughout his life he has always been surrounded by books. He taught himself four different languages and homeopathic medicine, even though these weren't related to his career in modern medicine. But he insists that all knowledge is relevant.

In the last years, reading has become my own favorite type of learning. I've found that it has a powerful effect in shaping my brain.

On a daily basis, I read for one to two hours. On weekends, I might read from four to five. I have read more than 1,000 books on business, health, and personal development since I started my company back in 1998. Each has helped me learn something unique and valuable. It will do the same for you.

When you read a book, you take yourself off to new and exciting places. You may learn advice from a well-respected CEO. You may travel on an adventure with a great safari hunter. You may find comfort and understanding, or learn the nuances of a new language or skill. You can go anywhere, be anyone.

The only way you'll be denied entry is if you do not pick up the book in the first place.

Read an hour per day to change your life.

I have carefully selected the following quotes and biographies of eleven successful people who have used reading to change their lives.

Reading-Related Quotes

Quotes and Biographies of Successful People Who Have Used
Reading to Change Their Lives

THOMAS JEFFERSON
(1743–1826)
THIRD PRESIDENT OF THE UNITED STATES OF AMERICA,

PRIMARY AUTHOR OF THE DECLARATION OF INDEPENDENCE

Jefferson was born into an affluent plantation family. He studied at the College of William and Mary, and then practiced law and served in local government. As a member of the Continental Congress, he drafted the Declaration of Independence at the age of 33. He was an advocate for separation of church and state, and in his home state of Virginia, he wrote a bill establishing freedom of religion.

After he left office, he sold his private collection of nearly 6,500 books—the best library in America—to the U.S. government. The 3,000-book collection of the Library of Congress had been burned by the British in the War of 1812, and Jefferson's collection gave it fresh life. His own interests were vast and were reflected in his private library. As a result, the Library of Congress became a library not just for the limited legislative needs of Congress, but for the broader needs of the nation.

I cannot live without books.

—Thomas Jefferson

ORHAN PAMUK
(b.1952)
AUTHOR & NOBEL PRIZE WINNER

ORHAN PAMUK learned his love of literature from his father, who would read aloud to the family with such sincerity that his children could not mistake how much he valued it. His father had a library of about 1,500 books. By the time Orhan was a teenager, he spent most of his time reading his father's books or buying his own at used bookshops. At the age of 22, he began writing, but his other pursuit was building his own library of Turkish and world literature. Over the years, his personal library grew to contain 12,000 books.

Pamuk's writings involve conflicted characters dealing with divided realities: the attraction and clash of eastern and western cultures, and of traditionalism and the modern world. Pamuk divides his time between Istanbul and New York City, where he teaches writing at Columbia University. His writings have been translated into 55 languages, and he was awarded the Nobel Prize for Literature in 2006.

I believe literature to be the most valuable hoard that humanity has gathered in its quest to understand itself.

—Orhan Pamuk

HARRY S. TRUMAN
(1884–1972)
33RD PRESIDENT OF THE UNITED STATES OF AMERICA

TRUMAN'S LOVE of reading, especially history books and literature, began as a boy. He said, "In reading the lives of great men, I found that the first victory they won was over themselves...self-discipline with all of them came first."

Truman saw action in France in WWI and rose to the rank of captain, earning the respect of his Missouri regiment. Active in the Democratic Party, he was elected to the U.S. Senate in 1934.

Truman gained prestige for his wartime Senate work investigating corruption. He was chosen to be FDR's running mate and became vice-president in January, 1945, unexpectedly becoming president when FDR died only eighty-two days later. Even more surprisingly, he won reelection four years later.

During Truman's first year in office, he managed the end of the war in Europe, the end of the war in Japan by means of the atomic bomb, and the founding of the U.N. His retirement was spent in reading and writing.

Not every reader is a leader, but every leader must be a reader.

—Harry S. Truman

HENRY FORD
(1863–1947)
INDUSTRIALIST & INVENTOR

HENRY FORD believed in learning by doing. He had little formal education but showed an early aptitude for machines. As a youngster, he took apart whatever he could manage in order to see how it worked. He built his first steam engine at age 15, and became an apprentice machinist at 16. He worked his way up to chief engineer with the Edison Illuminating Company. This position allowed him the financial freedom to experiment with his personal interest— internal combustion engines.

Ford is credited with introducing methods known in other industries—use of standardized parts and the assembly line—into the automobile industry. His invention of the movable assembly line lowered the cost of automobiles so much that the common workman could afford to buy one. The Model T fulfilled Ford's dream of creating a car for the masses.

Anyone who stops learning is old, whether at twenty or eighty.

—Henry Ford

ALDOUS HUXLEY
(1894–1963)
ENGLISH NOVELIST & CRITIC

ALDOUS HUXLEY was a lifelong learner and seeker of knowledge. He believed that reading was fundamental to self-improvement and growth. Huxley's favorite philosopher was the ancient Greek thinker Phyrro, who taught that we should not trust our senses or opinions. As a result, Huxley sought ways to expand the human experience beyond his five senses. He eventually turned to a form of Hinduism known as Vedanta, meditation, and mysticism.

In his later life, he gave lectures on how to develop human potential and is considered one of the founders of the Human Potential Movement. Huxley is best known for his novels *Brave New World*, warning of the dehumanizing effects of science and technology, and *Eyeless in Gaza*, in support of pacifism.

Every man who knows how to read has it in his power to magnify himself, to multiply the ways in which he exists, to make his life full, significant, and interesting.

—Aldous Huxley

ANTHONY TROLLOPE
(1815–1882)
ENGLISH NOVELIST

ANTHONY TROLLOPE had a goal, but it took him some time to formulate a plan. Trollope's mother had supported her family as a writer. Trollope wanted to be a writer, too, but because he had a regular job as a postal surveyor, he did not have time to devote to it. So he developed a concrete course of action: he established a firm schedule and quota for daily writing. Rather than wasting his travel time, he wrote regularly during the long train rides required for his job. He became very prolific, eventually writing 47 novels.

Thanks to a BBC television adaptation, Trollope's best-known novels in the US are the six Palliser novels, which are concerned with politics and the wealthy.

When Trollope passed away, he left his son an autobiography and two novels ready for sale and publication. He is considered one of the most important English novelists of the Victorian era.

The habit of reading is the only enjoyment in which there is no alloy; it lasts when all other pleasures fade.

—Anthony Trollope

DANIEL J. BOORSTIN
(1914–2004)
HISTORIAN & LIBRARIAN OF CONGRESS

AS A SOCIAL HISTORIAN, Daniel Boorstin knew that our history reveals ourselves. He won a 1974 Pulitzer Prize for his history book, *The Americans: The Democratic Experience*, but in total he wrote more than twenty books. Boorstin counseled that up-to-the-minute information was not the same as knowledge, and that not all information was worth knowing.

"The fog of information can drown out knowledge," he advised. He held that humanity's single greatest advance was creation of the book.

Boorstin was appointed the 12th Librarian of Congress by Gerald Ford and served from 1975 to 1987. He said his goal was "to humanize" the Library of Congress—the world's largest library—which he did by keeping the great bronze doors welcomingly open, setting up picnic tables and benches outside, and introducing lunchtime concerts.

By reading we discover our world, our history, and ourselves.

—Daniel J. Boorstin

E. B. WHITE
(1899–1985)
AMERICAN WRITER & PULITZER PRIZE WINNER

AS A CHILD, E.B. WHITE was so afraid of public speaking that if required to speak, he would write a speech and ask someone else to read it aloud for him. White graduated from Cornell and a few years later became a writer for *The New Yorker* magazine, where he met his wife, Katharine, literary editor of the magazine. They lived within literary circles with friends like Dorothy Parker and James Thurber.

In 1939, he moved to a farm in Maine, while continuing to write. In 1959, he revised his Cornell professor's book of principles of writing, which became the classic, Strunk and White, *The Elements of Style*, a basic handbook for writers. At the same time, he began writing his beloved children's books, *Stuart Little* (1945), *Charlotte's Web* (1952), and *The Trumpet of the Swan* (1970), which have started many children on the path of reading for pleasure. He received a special Pulitzer Prize for lifetime work in 1978.

Reading is the work of the alert mind, is demanding, and under ideal conditions produces finally a sort of ecstasy. This gives the experience of reading a sublimity and power unequalled by any other form of communication.

—E. B. White

ELIZABETH HARDWICK
(1916–2007)
WRITER AND CRITIC

EIGHTH IN A LINE of eleven children, Elizabeth Hardwick grew up while some of her older siblings were in college. This had an important influence upon her.

"The early days were dominated by love of reading, just reading, like eating, anything around."

Although born and educated in Kentucky, she aspired to be, as she put it, "a New York intellectual," so she entered a doctoral program in literature at Columbia University. She eventually dropped out, deciding that women in those days did not receive good teaching appointments. She started writing instead and became best known as a critical essayist, writing on anything cultural, from plays to literary figures. During the 1963 newspaper strike in New York City, when the weekly *New York Times Book Review* was absent for months on end, she, her husband (poet Robert Lowell), and a small group of friends, took the opportunity to found the *New York Review of Books*.

The greatest gift is a passion for reading. It is cheap, it consoles, it distracts, it excites, it gives you knowledge of the world and experience of a wide kind. It is a moral illumination.

—Elizabeth Hardwick

HORACE MANN
(1796–1859)
LAWYER & EDUCATIONAL REFORMER

HORACE MANN grew up on a farm and was able to attend regular school only sporadically. Much of his education came from books obtained from the town library. He nevertheless graduated Brown University and Litchfield Law School.

Like many progressives of the time, Mann believed in the perfectibility of people and society. He was an active supporter of contemporary social causes—temperance, abolitionism, women's suffrage, hospitals for the mentally ill—but education became the cause that was closest to his heart.

Mann believed that a democratic republic required an educated electorate. It was in the interest of the state to provide for the education of every child. Mann was an advocate of the Common School Movement, which championed universal, free, and non-sectarian public education. He helped bring about the first state law requiring compulsory attendance in school.

Resolve to edge in a little reading every day, if it is but a single sentence. If you gain 15 minutes a day, it will make itself felt at the end of the year.

—Horace Mann

JANE HAMILTON
(b. 1957)
AMERICAN AUTHOR

"I WAS OFTEN the worst in the thing that I loved to do: I was a lousy dancer, I had a weak voice in the choir, and in the theater group, because I couldn't act I did the backstage jobs. ... as a dead body during one performance, I started to laugh and could not stop. In short, I was ill-equipped to do much of anything. I studied English at Carleton College because I loved the freedom from the horrors of real life that a good book provides. ... I want there always to be a world in which people read books."

Hamilton was rejected from every writing program she applied to, and teachers told her it wasn't practical to expect to be able to write for a living. She did it anyway. Her first novel, *The Book of Ruth*, won the PEN/Ernest Hemingway Foundation award for best first novel and was an Oprah's Book Club selection. Her work deals with ordinary women in complex family situations.

It is books that are the key to the wide world; if you can't do anything else, read all that you can.

—Jane Hamilton

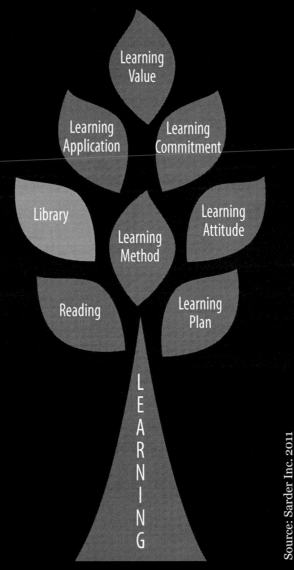

Learning
Value

Learning
Application

Learning
Commitment

Library

Learning
Method

Learning
Attitude

Reading

Learning
Plan

L
E
A
R
N
I
N
G

Steps to becoming a passionate lifelong learner

Source: Sarder Inc. 2011

STEP 7.
LIBRARY

Build Your Own Library.

Growing up in Bangladesh, reading and learning were favored endeavors for children, the equivalent of playing sports for an American boy. My parents understood that the benefits of reading were long lasting. Reading could change your future and broaden your possibilities.

I was happy to oblige. I loved to read and essentially grew up in the hospital library where my father was director, surrounded by knowledge. It was a library that my father had helped build for the hospital's employees and their children. It contained all kinds of books, but in those early years, encouraged by my father, I mostly read textbooks and memorized Bengali poetry. The beauty and lyricism of these poems have remained with me for over 30 years.

As I've grown into an adult, I've remembered that library as I've built my own. I've added libraries to both my home and office, so I can have access to the books that are important to me at any time.

By building a library, you have a personal collection of knowledge right at your fingertips. A library encourages you to return to a beloved book, to take notes for later reference, to make links between one idea and another.

We take for granted our access to the wealth of books and the wisdom contained within them, yet how fortunate we are! Libraries are vast repositories of knowledge. Whether it's poetry, history, or computer code, this is the information that teaches, inspires, and makes life meaningful.

This is a fortune that no one can take away from you.

I have carefully selected the following quotes and biographies of eight successful people who have built their own libraries.

LIBRARY-RELATED QUOTES

QUOTES AND BIOGRAPHIES OF SUCCESSFUL PEOPLE WHO HAVE BUILT THEIR OWN LIBRARIES

MARCUS TULLIUS CICERO
(106 BC–43 BC)
LEGAL ORATOR & PHILOSOPHER

AS A YOUNG MAN, Cicero chose as his motto "to always be the best and overtop the rest." He studied law, rhetoric, and philosophy, and then successfully ran for a succession of offices, each time at the youngest age allowable. He became known as one of Rome's greatest orators and prose writers.

Cicero wrote philosophy with the aim of helping those in power to make political decisions. He introduced the Romans to Greek philosophy and to the vocabulary of Latin philosophy. His letters and speeches are considered crucial sources for the final days of the Roman Republic.

St. Augustine and John Adams are numbered among the many who have read and studied Cicero throughout the centuries.

To add a library to a house is to give that house a soul.

—Marcus Tullius Cicero

ANATOLE FRANCE
(1844–1924)
NOBEL PRIZE WINNER IN LITERATURE

ANATOLE FRANCE (a pseudonym for Jacques Anatole Thibault) spent his entire life around books. His father was a Paris book dealer. Working in his father's shop, Anatole was exposed to important literary figures. He described the impact that living amidst the book stalls of old Paris had on him: "The passer-by who knows how to see always carries away some thought, as the bird flies off with a bit of straw for its nest."

France received a thorough classical education in Paris and then held a variety of jobs over the next two decades, but he always made time for writing. He continued to remain in bookish environments that supported his writing habit: he was a cataloguer and then a librarian. A prolific author, he wrote in nearly every genre. His complete works were compiled and published in twenty-five volumes, and he was awarded the Nobel Prize in Literature in 1921.

Never lend books, for no one ever returns them; the only books I have in my library are books that other people have lent me.

—Anatole France

AUGUSTINE BIRRELL
(1850–1933)
POLITICIAN, ESSAYIST, AND LITERARY CRITIC

AS A YOUNG LAW CLERK, Augustine Birrell was a member of the Liverpool Lyceum, a gentleman's club that housed Europe's first subscription lending library. His love of reading would later resurface when he wrote popular essays on his favorite literature.

Birrell eventually left his law practice to enter politics and held a number of British government posts, including President of the Board of Education. One of his greatest successes as Chief Secretary for Ireland was passage of the 1908 Irish Universities Bill, which created the National University of Ireland and Queen's University of Belfast. He was also known for his appealing sense of humor, which has been immortalized in his collections of essays. In Parliament, his wit and style were so distinctive that fellow politicians called his clever quips, "birrelling."

The man who has a library of his own collection is able to contemplate himself objectively, and is justified in believing in his own existence.

CHARLES WILLIAM ELIOT
(1834–1926)
PRESIDENT OF HARVARD UNIVERSITY

ELIOT BEGAN his career as a professor of math and chemistry at Harvard. When he was denied a reappointment to his position, he decided to study in Europe. During his two years there, he studied the organization of every aspect of the French and German educational systems. He believed in the utility of education and thought that European know-how could teach him how to transform American education so that it could produce the scientists and industrial leaders needed by the young country.

Eliot returned to the United States to assume a chemistry professorship at MIT, but it wasn't long before he was elected to be president of Harvard because of his liberal views on higher education. During his forty-year tenure as president, he transformed Harvard from a provincial college into a world-class research university. As a founding member of the College Entrance Examining Board, Eliot was a key figure in the creation of standardized admissions examinations.

One should get a first-class education from a shelf of books five feet long.

—Charles William Eliot

HENRY WARD BEECHER
(1813–1887)
ORATOR & CLERGYMAN

HENRY WARD BEECHER devoted his college time to studying subjects of personal interest, not just the required subjects. "I knew how to study, and I turned it upon what I wanted to know." What he wanted to know was how to speak and what to say, so he studied English classics, rhetoric, and oratory. Beecher recalled his purchase of his first books in college and observed that from that point on he no longer squandered money, because now he had a goal—building his library.

Beecher was the son of a minister and the brother of Harriet Beecher Stowe, author of *Uncle Tom's Cabin*. From his pulpit in the Plymouth Church in Brooklyn, he lectured on social and political issues, embracing most of the liberal causes of the time: women's suffrage, temperance, abolition, and evolutionism. His lectures were published weekly and read by people like the Illinois attorney Abraham Lincoln.

A little library, growing larger every year, is an honourable part of a man's history. It is a man's duty to have books. A library is not a luxury, but one of the necessaries of life.

—Henry Ward Beecher

JOHN RUSKIN
(1819–1900)
ART CRITIC AND SOCIAL COMMENTATOR

LIKE MANY of the Victorian era, John Ruskin was absorbed with nature. He was educated at home until he was 12, and his merchant father encouraged his only child's interest in botany, geology, and drawing. Ruskin was an avid reader of prose and poetry. His first prose work was published in the *Magazine of Natural History* when he was just 15. While still in his teens, he wrote *The Poetry of Architecture*, which argued that buildings should look like they belong in their environment and be built with local materials—ideas that look forward to today's environmental localism and naturalism in architecture.

Ruskin founded the Cambridge School of Art, which later became Anglia Ruskin University. In his writings, Ruskin often used first person and adopted the tone and position of a teacher. In his later writings, he turned to criticizing social ills, and he influenced the creation of Britain's Labour Party.

If a book is worth reading, it is worth buying.

—John Ruskin

THOMAS CARLYLE
(1795–1881)
SCOTTISH HISTORIAN & CRITIC

THOMAS CARLYLE walked the 80-odd miles from his village to the University of Edinburgh, which he attended for several years with the intent of becoming a minister. He left without a degree, however, and later gave up the idea of a life in the church because he no longer agreed with its teachings. He had begun studying German at the university and had done a great deal of independent reading. For a time, he made a living as a teacher and tutor, while gradually beginning to write.

Carlyle is known for introducing the work of German Romantic authors, such as Goethe and Schiller, to an English-speaking audience through his essays and translations. He also wrote a history of the French Revolution and a 6-volume history of Frederick the Great of Prussia, whom he greatly admired. Carlyle is credited with opening public discussion of the social problems of the Industrial Revolution and the gulf between rich and poor in England. He was the most respected social critic of Victorian-age England.

**The true university of these days is
a collection of books.**

—Thomas Carlyle

HOLBROOK JACKSON
(1874–1948)
WRITER & PUBLISHER

HOLBROOK JACKSON never attended college, but there was probably no one in England who loved books more than he did. He wrote that he was able to study while being part of the business world, only "by waging constant warfare with opposing circumstances; every studious hour a victory over the tyranny of business." Jackson published his first article at the age of 16, while working as a clerk. He later worked as a journalist and moved into the world of magazine publishing and editing, focusing principally on literary magazines. He helped found the Leeds Art Club, a focal point for modernist thought prior to WWI. He purchased his first magazine, *The New Age*, partly with the financial support of Irish playwright George Bernard Shaw.

Jackson wrote a large number of books and essays on literary subjects, love of books, book collecting, and book design and typography. He is credited with raising the standards of book production.

Your library is your portrait.

—Holbrook Jackson

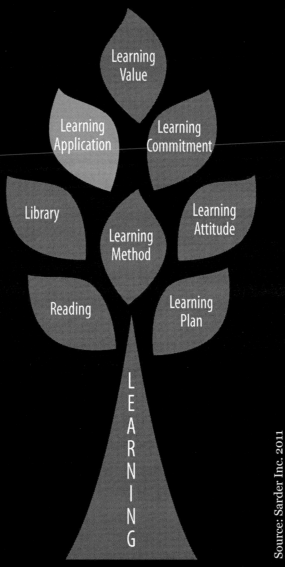

Steps to becoming a passionate lifelong learner

Source: Sarder Inc. 2011

STEP 8.
LEARNING APPLICATION

Apply What You Have Learned.

There is little point in developing a learning plan if you end up ignoring it; a book will do you no good if it gathers dust by your bedside. In order for the learning steps I've discussed to unleash their power, you need to apply them—consistently and with dedication. It's only through application that the fruits of your labor will become obvious.

I like this quote ascribed to the 19th century German poet Goethe:

"Whatever you can do or dream you can, begin it.

Boldness has genius, power and magic in it!"

I could not agree more.

One of my favorite books is Good to Great — Why Some Companies Make the Leap...and Others Don't, by Jim Collins. It's a bestseller, and I understand why.

In this book, Collins discusses three different questions that a company must be able to answer before it can become great.

First, a company must find out what it's best at; then, what drives its economic engine; and finally, what it's passionate about. When you can answer these three questions, you can take your business to the next level.

I answered these questions myself.

At Netcom Learning, what are we best at? Technology and business-related training for corporations and clients.

What are we passionate about? Promoting the value of lifelong learning.

What drives our economic engine? Revenue per hour.

When our company briefly went into the magazine business, I remembered Collins' book and his questions. They helped me realize that magazine publishing simply wasn't an area for which our company possessed   experience or passion. I'd learned a simple but profound lesson from Collins' book, and I was able to use it to shut down a business that wasn't profitable.

You can read books simply for enjoyment, but why not apply the knowledge they provide to improve your business and life?

I have carefully selected the following quotes and biographies of four successful people who have applied what they have learned.

Learning Application-Related Quotes

Quotes and Biographies of Successful People Who Have Applied What They Have Learned

DALE CARNEGIE
(1888–1955)
AUTHOR & MOTIVATIONAL SPEAKER

CARNEGIE GRADUATED from a Missouri teacher's college and embarked upon a career in sales. He had aspirations to be an adult education teacher, but in thinking about what he wanted to teach, he realized that his most helpful college class had been in public speaking. It had given him the confidence to operate in the business world.

He convinced the Y.M.C.A. to allow him to teach public speaking courses on a commission only basis. Over time, his classes grew to be wildly successful, and an unexpected career was launched. Carnegie offered courses on effective speaking, human relations, and salesmanship.

Today, the company he started still offers training in more than 80 countries and 25 languages. His bestselling book, *How to Win Friends and Influence People*, continues to find an audience.

Learning is an active process. We learn by doing. Only knowledge that is used sticks in your mind.

—Dale Carnegie

ANTON CHEKHOV
(1860–1904)
AUTHOR

CHEKHOV IS CONSIDERED the father of the modern short story and play. As a schoolboy, he enjoyed acting in amateur plays and attending the provincial theater. His mother had a gift for storytelling, and she was the one who first taught him to read and write.

The family struggled financially, but Chekhov was able to earn a scholarship to Moscow University to study medicine. He first began writing to help support his parents and siblings. In those early days, he called medicine "his wife," and writing, "his mistress." He practiced medicine throughout his life, often treating peasants without charge, and he also built three schools for them from his own funds.

By the end of his life, he had written four plays that are considered classics, and over 200 short stories.

Knowledge is of no value unless you put it into practice.

—Anton Chekhov

GLORIA STEINEM
(b. 1934)
FEMINIST ACTIVIST, LECTURER, WRITER, AND EDITOR

GLORIA STEINEM studied government at Smith College. Upon graduation, she spent two years on a fellowship in India, where she was influenced by the peaceful activism of Ghandi and developed a more global perspective. She became a freelance journalist, participating in the founding of *New York* magazine, for which she was a political columnist. During that time, she became active in supporting political candidates and leftist causes.

Steinem's interest in feminism was sparked when, as a journalist, she attended a meeting of a women's liberation group called the Redstockings, and was moved by the women's stories she heard there. In 1972 she co-founded *Ms.*, the first magazine in the nation to be run by women. She served as one of its editors for fifteen years. Her books include *Revolution from Within: A Book of Self-Esteem*.

The first problem for all of us, men and women, is not to learn , but to unlearn.

—Gloria Steinem

HENRY DAVID THOREAU
(1817–1862)
NATURALIST AND WRITER

HENRY DAVID THOREAU lived a life of commitment. A staunch abolitionist, he was an energetic member of the Underground Railroad. He went to jail rather than pay taxes, as a show of conscientious objection to the Mexican-American War, which could have extended slavery into new territories. To his annoyance, his aunt paid the taxes for him, so he spent only one night in jail. The outcome of the experience, however, was his groundbreaking work, *Civil Disobedience*, which has inspired political and social activists from Martin Luther King, Jr. to Gandhi.

Thoreau also spent two years in a self-made house at Walden Pond, conducting an experiment in living simply in solitary contemplation of nature. His writings from this experience resulted in his famous book *Walden*. His views on the relationship of people and nature were key in the movement to preserve parks and promote environmentalism.

A truly great book teaches me better than to read it. I must soon lay it down, and commence living on its hint...What I began by reading, I must finish by acting.

—Henry David Thoreau

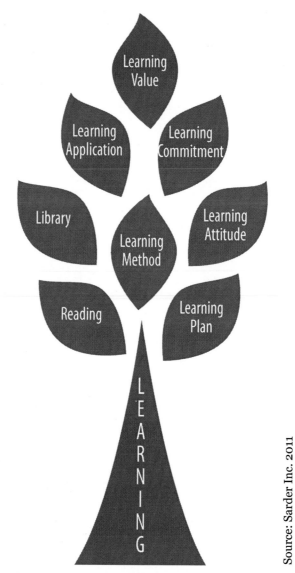

Steps to becoming a passionate lifelong learner

Source: Sarder Inc. 2011

Steps to Becoming a Passionate Lifelong Learner

Learning Value — Appreciate the value of attaining continuous knowledge.

Learning Commitment — Embrace being a committed lifelong learner.

Learning Attitude — Develop the right attitude towards continuous learning.

Learning Plan — Develop an effective learning plan to excel in your field.

Learning Method — Become an effective learner by combining a variety of learning methods.

Reading — Read an hour each day and grow wealthy.

Library — Build your own library.

Learning Application — Apply what you have learned.

Source: Sarder Inc. 2011

Join Us in the Learning Movement

I am excited to share with you my powerful program for becoming a lifelong learner.

The great benefit of continuous learning is that it's available to everyone. It's the most democratic of life's endeavors and requires no special equipment or unusual talent. Learning should be fun!

Starting today, implement each learning step towards becoming a passionate lifelong learner into your life, and you'll be on your way to personal and professional transformation.

Now that you're inspired, here are some ways to remain energized for the long haul:

1. **Become a passionate Lifelong Learner**
   a. Develop and implement a dynamic learning plan (Learning Goal, Competency Method, Learning Methods).
   b. Read an hour each day.
   c. Build your own library.
   d. Start or join a book club.

2. **Promote the value of lifelong learning**

   Whether you are a politician, CEO, teacher, student, journalist, or other professional, The Learning Movement believes in sharing and passing along inspiration and resources:
   a. Readers: Distribute the "Gift of Learning: The Learning Map" cards to eight people you care about the most.
   b. CEOs, Managers, Leaders: Build a culture of learning within your company by distributing this book. The best-run organization is a learning organization.
   c. Business Owners / Entrepreneurs: Become avid readers and passionate lifelong learners if you want to run a successful business. Begin to promote a culture of learning by practicing the lessons in this book.

d. Journalist, Activist: Use your authority to promote the value of lifelong learning. Talk about the ideas in this book to create a buzz about a new learning movement.

e. Congressman, Politicians: Develop a continuous learning culture in the United States. Education begins after we finish our schooling, through self-education for adults.

f. Educators, Teachers, Professors: Make this book required reading if you want your students to become self-learners in the future.

The Learning Movement's motto is: Learning is Cool! Join us in The Learning Movement right now!

THE GIFT OF LEARNING: THE LEARNING MAP

Steps to Becoming a Passionate Lifelong Learner

LEARNING VALUE	— Appreciate the value of attaining continuous knowledge.
LEARNING COMMITMENT	— Embrace being a committed lifelong learner.
LEARNING ATTITUDE	— evelop the right attitude to continuous learning.
LEARNING PLAN	— Develop an effective learning plan to excel in your field.
LEARNING METHOD	— Become an effective learner by combining a variety of learning methods.
READING	— Read an hour each day and grow wealthy.
LIBRARY	— Build your own library.
LEARNING APPLICATION	— Apply what you have learned.

Learning: Steps to Becoming a Passionate Lifelong Learner, 2011
www.russellsarder.com

Steps to Becoming a Passionate Lifelong Learner

LEARNING VALUE	— Appreciate the value of attaining continuous knowledge.
LEARNING COMMITMENT	— Embrace being a committed lifelong learner.
LEARNING ATTITUDE	— evelop the right attitude to continuous learning.
LEARNING PLAN	— Develop an effective learning plan to excel in your field.
LEARNING METHOD	— Become an effective learner by combining a variety of learning methods.
READING	— Read an hour each day and grow wealthy.
LIBRARY	— Build your own library.
LEARNING APPLICATION	— Apply what you have learned.

Learning: Steps to Becoming a Passionate Lifelong Learner, 2011
www.russellsarder.com

Steps to Becoming a Passionate Lifelong Learner

LEARNING VALUE	— Appreciate the value of attaining continuous knowledge.
LEARNING COMMITMENT	— Embrace being a committed lifelong learner.
LEARNING ATTITUDE	— evelop the right attitude to continuous learning.
LEARNING PLAN	— Develop an effective learning plan to excel in your field.
LEARNING METHOD	— Become an effective learner by combining a variety of learning methods.
READING	— Read an hour each day and grow wealthy.
LIBRARY	— Build your own library.
LEARNING APPLICATION	— Apply what you have learned.

Learning: Steps to Becoming a Passionate Lifelong Learner, 2011
www.russellsarder.com

Steps to Becoming a Passionate Lifelong Learner

LEARNING VALUE	— Appreciate the value of attaining continuous knowledge.
LEARNING COMMITMENT	— Embrace being a committed lifelong learner.
LEARNING ATTITUDE	— evelop the right attitude to continuous learning.
LEARNING PLAN	— Develop an effective learning plan to excel in your field.
LEARNING METHOD	— Become an effective learner by combining a variety of learning methods.
READING	— Read an hour each day and grow wealthy.
LIBRARY	— Build your own library.
LEARNING APPLICATION	— Apply what you have learned.

Learning: Steps to Becoming a Passionate Lifelong Learner, 2011
www.russellsarder.com

Steps to Becoming a Passionate Lifelong Learner

LEARNING VALUE	— Appreciate the value of attaining continuous knowledge.
LEARNING COMMITMENT	— Embrace being a committed lifelong learner.
LEARNING ATTITUDE	— evelop the right attitude to continuous learning.
LEARNING PLAN	— Develop an effective learning plan to excel in your field.
LEARNING METHOD	— Become an effective learner by combining a variety of learning methods.
READING	— Read an hour each day and grow wealthy.
LIBRARY	— Build your own library.
LEARNING APPLICATION	— Apply what you have learned.

Learning: Steps to Becoming a Passionate Lifelong Learner, 2011
www.russellsarder.com

Steps to Becoming a Passionate Lifelong Learner

LEARNING VALUE	— Appreciate the value of attaining continuous knowledge.
LEARNING COMMITMENT	— Embrace being a committed lifelong learner.
LEARNING ATTITUDE	— evelop the right attitude to continuous learning.
LEARNING PLAN	— Develop an effective learning plan to excel in your field.
LEARNING METHOD	— Become an effective learner by combining a variety of learning methods.
READING	— Read an hour each day and grow wealthy.
LIBRARY	— Build your own library.
LEARNING APPLICATION	— Apply what you have learned.

Learning: Steps to Becoming a Passionate Lifelong Learner, 2011
www.russellsarder.com

Steps to Becoming a Passionate Lifelong Learner

LEARNING VALUE	— Appreciate the value of attaining continuous knowledge.
LEARNING COMMITMENT	— Embrace being a committed lifelong learner.
LEARNING ATTITUDE	— evelop the right attitude to continuous learning.
LEARNING PLAN	— Develop an effective learning plan to excel in your field.
LEARNING METHOD	— Become an effective learner by combining a variety of learning methods.
READING	— Read an hour each day and grow wealthy.
LIBRARY	— Build your own library.
LEARNING APPLICATION	— Apply what you have learned.

Learning: Steps to Becoming a Passionate Lifelong Learner, 2011
www.russellsarder.com

Steps to Becoming a Passionate Lifelong Learner

LEARNING VALUE	— Appreciate the value of attaining continuous knowledge.
LEARNING COMMITMENT	— Embrace being a committed lifelong learner.
LEARNING ATTITUDE	— evelop the right attitude to continuous learning.
LEARNING PLAN	— Develop an effective learning plan to excel in your field.
LEARNING METHOD	— Become an effective learner by combining a variety of learning methods.
READING	— Read an hour each day and grow wealthy.
LIBRARY	— Build your own library.
LEARNING APPLICATION	— Apply what you have learned.

Learning: Steps to Becoming a Passionate Lifelong Learner, 2011
www.russellsarder.com

"The moment you think you know it all, you stop growing. Develop the passion for learning; be a lifelong learner."

—Russell Sarder,
Chairman & CEO, Sarder Inc.

ABOUT THE AUTHOR

An entrepreneur who inherited his passion for lifelong learning from his parents, Russell Sarder founded NetCom Learning (www. NetComLearning.com) in 1998. Sarder has led NetCom Learning to be recognized as a technical and business training leader. Within a decade, he has grown it into an multimillion revenue business. Sarder has been selected as a winner of the 2011 Top Ten Asian American Business Awards.

Driven by his passion and dedication, and differentiated by its focus on client excellence, NetCom Learning has successfully aligned itself with industry leaders, such as Project Management Institute, Microsoft, CISCO, CompTia, EC-Council, Autodesk, Adobe, Check Point, Novell, Oracle, and IBM.

NetCom Learning was listed as one of the fastest growing private companies in the United States by Inc 5000 Magazine in 2008. NetCom

Learning also received the CPLS of the Year 2007 award by Microsoft, and the EC-Council Circle of Excellence award in 2010.

Sarder is also Chairman and CEO of Sarder Inc., a holding company that includes NetCom Learning, NetCom CMS (Central Management Software), Ebiz9, Technology and Training magazine, and other smaller companies. Microsoft Chairman Bill Gates, Microsoft CEO Steve Ballmer, CISCO CEO John Chambers have contributed to his technology magazine.

Sarder is the creator of Netcom Learning's Sarder Scholarship Program, awarded monthly to an ambitious individual who wishes either to begin or advance an IT career.

Sarder is a frequent speaker on topics of learning culture and business management. As a motivational speaker, he has appeared in newspaper reports in the Daily News, the New York Times, and the New York Post. His TV appearances include CBS Market Watch, Yahoo Finance and New York One. Sarder has also spoken at major industry events organized by CompTia, Microsoft, and NetCom Learning.

Sarder is an avid reader and passionate lifelong learner who has followed in the footsteps of his father. A denizen of New York City, Sarder also lives a healthy lifestyle and writes learning books in his spare time.

About NetCom Learning

At NetCom Learning, we are passionate about learning. We are passionate about making businesses and individuals more productive and competitive by empowering them with knowledge.

Purpose: NetCom Learning exists to promote the value of lifelong learning.

Values: Our core values are integrity, success, trust, respect, and excellence.

Mission: Our mission is to grow the company profitably every year by becoming the most respected and trusted Learning Organization.

NetCom Learning is a premier provider of IT and business training solutions to companies, individuals, and government agencies. Since its inception in 1998, NetCom has trained over 90% of the Fortune 500, serviced over 22,000 business customers, and advanced the skills of more than 50,000 professionals through its hands-on, expert-led training courses. Recognized by Microsoft as its Worldwide Training Partner of the Year and named to the Inc. 5000 Fastest Growing Private Companies in America, NetCom is proud of its reputation as a top-quality learning organization. NetCom Learning, headquartered in New York, has three main campus locations and over 20 satellite locations worldwide and counting.

NetCom Learning
Phone (866) 563-8266
Fax (646) 292-5170
Email marketing@netcomlearning.com
20 West 33rd Street, 4th Floor
New York, NY 10001
www.netcomlearning.com

Campus Locations
New York City | 20 West 33rd Street 4th Floor | New York, NY 10001
Las Vegas, Nevada | 5051 Duke Ellington Way | Las Vegas, NV 89119
Sterling, Virginia | 22685 Holiday Park Drive Suite 60 | Sterling, VA 20166

ABOUT SARDER INC.

Sarder Inc. is passionately committed to  helping its portfolio companies succeed. We know that it takes more than solid financial support to get a company off the ground. We help make things happen. We deeply believe that teams can win.

Entrepreneurs gain access to our matched portfolio of companies and associations with global business leaders. These relationships are the foundation for strategic alliances, partnership opportunities, and the sharing of insights to help build new ventures faster, broader, and with less risk.

Since 1998, we have co-founded, funded, and supported many successful companies in many business areas.

Major Sarder Portfolio Companies	Business Area
NetCom Learning	Training
Technology and Training Magazine	Publishing
Sarder Consulting	Consulting
Sarder Press	Publishing

For more information, please visit www.sarder.com or email russell@netcomlearning.com.

Sarder Inc.
20 west 33rd street 4F
New York City, NY 10001
www.sarder.com